Praise for *The Invitation*

"*The Invitation* is a treasure. If you want to live more deeply, honestly, and passionately, you must read this book."

—Richard Carlson, author of *Don't Sweat the Small Stuff*

"A remarkable book . . . A fierce and tender presence, its wisdom could become a lifelong companion, engaging and awakening the original and unique rhythm of your mind and soul."

—John O'Donohue, author of *Anam Cara*

Praise for *The Dance*

"This book is a blessing, a healing, a reminder to stop living in the neighborhood of your self and go home at last."

—Rachel Naomi Remen, M.D., author of *Kitchen Table Wisdom* and *My Grandfather's Blessings*

"To read *The Dance* is to invite all of the far-flung parts of yourself . . . back onto the dance floor for a slow and sweet waltz. At the end of the dance, you have whirled yourself back into one whole person."

—Elizabeth Lesser, author of *The Seeker's Guide*

Praise for *The Call*

"Fiercely, courageously, honestly, *The Call* reaches down to the tender heart of what it means to be human."

—Roger Housden, author of *10 Poems to Change Your Life* and *10 Poems to Open Your Heart*

"Once in a great while a book is like a living being. It takes up residence inside you, and speaks with a voice that is strong and true, long after you've closed the cover. Its wisdom becomes your own, a gentle and profound awakening that keeps coming to you, again and again. *The Call* is one of those rare and precious books. It is a gift to us all from a wise, funny, and honest teacher who knows the territory of the human heart and soul like few others."

—Joan Borysenko, Ph.D., author of
A Woman's Journey to God and *Inner Peace for Busy Women*

Opening
The
Invitation

Opening
THE
INVITATION

The Poem That Has
Touched Lives
Around the World

Oriah Mountain Dreamer

HarperCollins*Publishers*Ltd

Opening The Invitation
© 2004 by Mountain Dreaming Productions. All rights reserved.

Published by HarperCollins Publishers Ltd

First Edition

HarperCollins books may be purchased for educational, business,
or sales promotional use through our Special Markets Department.

HarperCollins Publishers Ltd
2 Bloor Street East, 20th Floor
Toronto, Ontario, Canada
M4W 1A8

www.harpercanada.ca

National Library of Canada Cataloguing in Publication is available

ISBN 0-00-200785-1

PCC 9 8 7 6 5 4 3 2 1

Printed and bound in the United States

With gratitude to my parents

Don and Carolyn House

THE
INVITATION

It doesn't interest me
what you do for a living.
I want to know what you ache for
and if you dare to dream
of meeting your heart's longing.

It doesn't interest me how old you are.
I want to know if you will risk
    looking like a fool
for love

for your dream
for the adventure of being alive.

It doesn't interest me what planets are
        squaring your moon . . .
I want to know if you have touched
        the center of your own sorrow
if you have been opened by life's
        betrayals   [7]
or have become shriveled and closed
        from fear of further pain.

I want to know if you can sit with
        pain
mine or your own
without moving to hide it
or fade it
or fix it.

I want to know if you can be
        with joy
mine or your own
if you can dance with wildness
and let the ecstasy fill you to the
        tips of your
fingers and toes
without cautioning us to
be careful
be realistic
to remember the limitations of
        being human.

It doesn't interest me if the story you
    are telling me is true.
I want to know if you can disappoint
    another
to be true to yourself.

If you can bear the accusation of
    betrayal
and not betray your own soul.
If you can be faithless
and therefore trustworthy.

I want to know if you can see beauty
even when it is not pretty
every day.
And if you can source your own life
from its presence.

I want to know if you can live with
        failure,
yours or mine,
and still stand on the edge of the lake
and shout to the silver of the full
        moon,
"Yes!"

It doesn't interest me
to know where you live or how much
        money you have.
I want to know if you can get up
after the night of grief and despair
weary and bruised to the bone
and do what needs to be done
to feed the children.

It doesn't interest me who you know
or how you came to be here.
I want to know if you will stand
in the center of the fire

with me
and not shrink back.

It doesn't interest me where or what
        or with whom
you have studied.
I want to know what sustains you
from the inside
when all else falls away.

I want to know if you can be alone
with yourself
and if you truly like the company
        you keep
in the empty moments.   [23]

Opening
THE
INVITATION

Writing
"The Invitation"

SOME DAYS THINGS UNFOLD IN
my life in a way that make me wonder why I am so certain that I need to dili-
gently plan and work and try to make things
come out right. Oh, I'm not suggesting
that planning and working don't sometimes
pay off, don't sometimes render hoped-for
results. But when you follow the impulse that
comes from a deep stillness without the

smallest thought or a shadow of an expectation about the outcome and then watch as things effortlessly unfold in a way you would not even have dared imagine, it makes you question all this trying, this dark certainty that everything must be earned or fought for. It makes you consider grace and the blessings of a human life that are ours simply by virtue of being alive. It opens you to the possibility of real surprises. It reminds you of how limited our perspective is, of how we often can't even imagine what is possible as we take a deep breath and plunge into another day, throwing a load of laundry into the dryer and stacking dirty dishes in the sink as we rush to make the morning bus, juggling deadlines at work against parent-teacher interviews, cringing as we vow once again that this will be the last time we pick up fast food or order pizza for dinner.

"The Invitation" came in a quiet
moment late at night when
tiredness stopped my head from
censoring the words that flowed
from my heart onto the page.

But sometimes, unexpectedly, a quiet moment finds us and we drop down into the life we have beneath all the rushing and the trying and the endless daily details, sinking into the fertile soil of the sometimes neglected inner life, where the seeds of remembering what matters are planted. What comes from that place when we give it half a chance flowers in our lives and the world, creating unexpected changes in the direction of our journey and offering unanticipated blessings to us and those around us.

This is what writing "The Invitation" was like for me. It came in a quiet moment late at night when tiredness stopped my head from censoring the words that flowed from my heart onto the page. I had just returned from a party. I'm not good at parties. I always feel slightly confused standing around talking to strangers about things that don't really matter. I can't quite figure out what it is

[30]

we're supposed to be doing. If we are celebrating something, someone's birthday or graduation or retirement, I want to do something together that will mark the occasion, have people offer prayers or stories or meditations that bring us into mindful awareness of the occasion and the person we are there to celebrate. And if we are just there to get to know each other, then I want to talk about things that matter, want to know how others feel about their daily lives, want to hear their hopes and disappointments, want to know what they think about just before they fall asleep at night, how they feel when their alarm clocks pull them up out of dreams in the morning. I'm not suggesting that my attitude toward parties is necessarily a good one. At times I wish I understood the purpose and practice of just hanging out with others, but the whole thing eludes me. I'd rather take a walk in the woods or read a good book or have a hot bath. So most of the time I just don't go to parties.

But once in a while I worry a little about my inability to happily participate in what appear to be normal social activities. On this particular night, feeling this worry niggling at me, I'd convinced myself to go to the party, inwardly berating myself, "Oh, for crying out loud, Oriah, just go to the party and try to be normal for a change. Not every moment has to be deeply meaningful and spiritually insightful! Just try chatting with people."

But it didn't work. Oh, it was a perfectly ordinary party and I'd done my best to behave myself, chatted with people without asking for or offering more than what was expected. But the familiar boredom mixed with confusion and frustration had once again set in as people stood around, drinks in hand, asking and answering the usual questions: What do you do? Where do you live? Who do you know? So I'd come home tired and disgruntled, more dissatisfied with social norms than with my own inability or unwillingness to conform to them.

Although this dissatisfaction with small talk is something that has always been with me, there was a reason why the feeling was so acute on this particular night in May of 1994. One year earlier on this day, standing in my kitchen cleaning and chatting with my dear friend Catherine, I'd watched as she'd suddenly raised her hand to her head, complaining of a sharp pain. And as she'd winced I'd seen a flash of light, like the blinding pop of a camera's flashbulb, next to her temple. I can't explain it. Perhaps it was because my grandfather had had an aneurysm years before that the word immediately came into my mind like a silent and certain shadow filling me with dread.

There are events by which we mark our lives, usually unexpected and often tragic occurrences beyond our control that become a kind of watershed, all other events becoming known as that which came before or after. In North America Kennedy's assassination and September 11 are two such moments in our collective history. That day with Catherine became one of those reference points in my life. As I drove her to the hospital and she stopped breathing, as I reached out for her crying her name, as I sat in the hospital waiting room listening to the surgeon telling me he did not think he could save her, I felt everything I thought I knew turn to ash. A brain aneurysm is usually fatal and almost always unanticipated. One minute everything is as it has been, and in the next everything is changed forever. Being with Catherine that day abruptly ended any temptation I'd ever felt to buy into comforting

New Age platitudes that promise unlimited control over our lives or pretend that we can know with certainty that everything happens—is caused or orchestrated by a higher power—for a worthy reason. It ripped from my hands and my heart my unacknowledged and only semiconscious belief in the power of my own will to protect myself and those I love from any real harm through hard work and diligent practice. It brought the reality of impermanence, the reality of our own mortality and the consistency and unpredictability of change in our lives, up against my face—hard. If I wanted to live fully I had to learn how to keep my heart open while remaining conscious of the enormity of what I cannot know and what I cannot control no matter how hard I work.

Catherine lived. Today she resides in a group home where she can receive the care she needs, continually working to improve

I was filled with wanting to
make sure I did not waste one
moment on that which does not
matter, on small talk that does
not really share anything or
create any intimacy between us.

her physical mobility and mental acuity. Despite her disabilities and all she has lost, she continually expresses her gratitude for being alive.

One of the many things I received from that day with Catherine was a heightened sense of how none of us knows how much time we have. Any one of us could be, in this moment, sixty seconds or an hour away from a brain aneurysm. With this realization came a deepening of my desire to be fully present for every moment of this precious life I have been given. On the first anniversary of that day with Catherine, on the night I wrote "The Invitation," I was filled with wanting to make sure I did not waste one moment on that which does not matter, on small talk that does not really share anything or create any intimacy between us. Being with Catherine on that day a year before had split me open to my own longing to live from a deeper place, had given me the courage to allow the voice of what I ache for have its say.

So I sat down to write at my desk in the dim light of the street lamp outside my window. Since I was a child I have written to understand myself and the world, to find the stories that show me the meaning I can make of my life. I write as a way of finding and being with what is within and around me, a way of connecting to that which is larger than it all. On this night I used a writing exercise I had received from poet David Whyte at a workshop over a year before. David had given workshop participants a writing exercise based on his poem "Self Portrait" from his poetry collection *Fire in the Earth,* asking us to begin with the phrase "It doesn't interest me . . ." and continue with "What I really want . . ." I had used this writing exercise dozens of times to go deeper in both my writing and my meditations, to discover what

I did not know about my own thoughts and feelings, to open to the ache I felt in my chest for something more.

As the words flowed I recognized a voice that has always been there within me: the voice that passionately seeks life's purpose; the voice of the tired heart that longs for real intimacy and deep rest; the voice that asks me to be fully present with it all—the pain and the joy, the beauty and the sorrow, the inner silence and the noise of the world. I wasn't the only one who recognized this voice as part of who I had always been. Later, after the prose poem had become the book *The Invitation,* I received a letter from Jeff, a man I'd met when we were both teenagers on a canoe trip in Algonquin Park in northern Ontario. Paddling together through the wilderness in the same canoe for two weeks, we had become each other's first love but had lost touch in the intervening thirty years.

Finding my name and the prose poem on the Internet, he wrote to me, telling me he recognized "the same tone of voice, the same clear thought that made my heart soar before I even knew what to do about it . . ." all those years ago. It has been three years since I received this letter from Jeff. We were married eight months ago, and Jeff says he is grateful to love and live with the only woman he knows who came with her own manual.

When I meet people at bookstore events they often ask me about my background. They want to know where the voice of "The Invitation" came from, what gave me enough faith in the longing to let it speak unfettered. I think we all have this voice and are given an underlying faith in its wisdom as our birthright. It is what gently prods us to remember that life is about more than just continuing. It is what calls us to be all of what and who we are in terms defined by our own soul's knowing instead of molding ourselves according to the culturally sanctioned drive for material success or a particular tradition's or teacher's definition of spiritual enlightenment. Each of us has this voice, although how it speaks to us, the words it uses, will differ and be shaped by the particular circumstances of our lives. I will tell you here a little of what I know about the shaping of this woman. You probably have at least one question if not a few qualms about the unusual name I use. So let this be the thread we follow into the story that has been woven from my life.

The truth is, I never intended to go into the world using the name Oriah Mountain Dreamer, and I confess I too think, "Flaky!" when someone approaches me and tells me her name is something like "Ophelia Morning Glory" or "Azaria Thornbird." Pretty cheeky for a woman walking around using the name Oriah Mountain Dreamer! But then, if you had told me twenty-five years ago that I would study with and apprentice to a Native American shaman, I would have thought that sounded crazy. But in 1985 I went to northern Ontario to meet a visiting shaman who was offering a week of traditional spiritual teachings and ceremonial healings. Suffering from chronic illness, married with two young sons, and living on very little income, I found the logistical arrangements and finances for the trip almost impossible. But I had been consistently ill since the birth of my second son two years earlier. While the medical profession had just begun to talk about something called chronic fatigue syndrome and was investigating the possibility of a viral cause, it had no real treatment for the debilitating fatigue and constant infections that my failing immune system could not fight off. I was desperate.

I was also afraid: afraid I would not be well enough after the journey to the northern retreat center to even participate in the week's activities; afraid it would not do any good, that I would find no healing there but would continue to be ill and unable to function normally for the rest of my life; afraid that the healing would work but that it would require something of me, would call for difficult choices in my life.

As I try to choose the events in my life that have shaped the voice heard in "The Invitation," those years of illness would have to top the list. Lying in bed with a fever, exhausted but unable to find the rest my body needed, trying to soften to the pain in my legs and arms, feeling as if my muscles were being pulled from my bones, I began to learn about the power of the breath and the limits of my will. And in some ways, when the weeks of acute illness passed and I moved

It was a good life. It just was

not my life, the life my soul

intended or needed to live.

into months of chronic infections and constant fatigue, it was harder. Stumbling through days when all I wanted to do was sleep, unable to think clearly but needing to take care of my children, I began to consider that something at the core of my life, something essential to who I was, was "off." I think I knew even before I went to see the shaman that the root cause of my illness— and here I am not denying the reality of viruses or constitutional weaknesses but looking for the deeper causes that make us susceptible to both—was an inner disease with the life I was living. It was a good life. It just was not *my* life, the life my soul intended or needed to live. I had not yet understood that the desire to live connected to a daily sense of the sacred presence and meaning within and around me, a desire that had been with me from my earliest memories, had to be shaped by the particular strengths and weaknesses, preferences and needs of an individual woman. I had to give up my ideal, the notion that if I were living from the center of my spirituality I could thrive under any circumstances, and live with the real, the need to choreograph my choices according to what one small human woman—me— needed to maintain her balance, sustain her happiness, and cultivate her daily conscious connection to that which was larger than herself.

The shaman spent an hour alone with me. He asked me to tell him my story. I told him what I knew. And at the end of the hour, after doing a few minutes of healing touch on my arms and legs, he told me to feel the power I had to make the choices that would enable me to stay connected to my own life, replenish my energy, and follow my dreams. He stated this with great certainty and simplicity, without drama or emphasis, and I recognized it as something I already knew. It was as if someone had switched on a light that had been accidentally turned off. I left his small cabin to go out into the wilderness to do the ceremony of fasting and praying that he had given to me, feeling more awake and energized than I had in years. From that moment on, my health began to stabilize and the illness I had suffered dissipated. He gave me a medicine name, the name that tells the world something about why a person is here and what they have to offer, and told me that *Mountain Dreamer* meant "one who likes to push the edge and can help others do the same." At the time, my idea of pushing the edge was staying up until 9 p.m. I assumed that pushing the edge would mean challenging myself to find the energy to do and learn and be more. But for some of us—particularly those of us susceptible to illnesses like chronic fatigue because we do too much— pushing the edge is more about consciously stopping, about finding deep stillness and rest and peace, less about doing and more about being. But it would be years before I understood this small and difficult truth.

With my health returning, I began to make hard choices that created change in my life and the lives of those around me: I left my marriage and the community in which my husband and I had participated for many years; eventually I left the work I was doing as a social worker to share the spiritual teachings I continued to learn with this shaman, a choice that allowed me to work out of my home and be there with my sons before and after school. For the next fifteen years I made a modest living teaching classes and leading spiritual retreats, taking people out to experience the ceremonies I continued to do for myself, ceremonies of fasting and praying alone in the wilderness. Within this ceremonial context and in the writing I did for the newsletter that was sent to students, I used my medicine name, Oriah Mountain Dreamer. Elsewhere in my daily life, I used my family name, House, although it caused problems when people receiving messages from "Oriah House" assumed it was some kind of group home or social agency.

It is startling now to see how much the path of my life was shaped by the illness that developed when I was thirty years old. Of course, many people, even many who are desperately ill, would not consider going to a Native American shaman for a healing, let alone taking themselves out into the wilderness to fast and pray and then follow the directions indicated by the guidance that comes from the deep silence and solitude. In fact, when I had first received a notice in the mail

I am an ordinary woman
with an extraordinary hunger,
an ache to discover and
consciously live the meaning
of my life.

telling me that this shaman was coming to Ontario and would be doing healings, I could not bring myself to go see him. It all just seemed too weird. But when he returned a year later, my fear of the continuing illness was greater than my fear of doing something weird. Everything within me seemed to be gently prodding me in the direction of going to see this healer: the medical profession's inability to come up with a solution to my failing health; my dreams of a group of old women I had come to call the Grandmothers, who had come to me in my sleep for many years, who told me now to make the journey, to see this shaman; my tendency since childhood to look for the deeper causes of things in spiritual teaching within and outside traditional religious beliefs and practices.

The truth is that I am an ordinary woman with an extraordinary hunger, an ache to discover and consciously live the meaning of my life, and a conviction that that hunger can only be satisfied by cultivating a deeply spiritual life.

This hunger was there when I was a teenager. When other girls were completely preoccupied with good grades, hairstyles, makeup, and dating, I was corralling my classmates into loosely organized discussion groups about theology and ethics, obsessed with understanding what God was and how we could know God's will in matters of conscience and social justice. Don't get me wrong—I was a diligent student. I got good grades and wanted to wear the latest outfits and have the right shade of turquoise eye shadow and white lipstick and be asked to go to the movies by some tall, awkward teenage boy as much as the next girl. It was the early seventies. I streaked my hair a lighter shade of blond, rolled up my waistband to meet the ever-rising standards for miniskirts, and pulled on my high white boots just like everyone else. But no matter how much I wanted to fit in, I just couldn't quite pull it off, couldn't stop asking people why they thought they were here, how they prayed when they were alone, or what they wanted to do with their lives to make the world a better place. These kinds of questions do not tend to inspire most teenage boys to ask a girl out on a date.

These questions are the kinds of things Jeff was remembering when he said in his note that the voice in "The Invitation" was the voice of the girl he knew thirty years before. I was then and remain today somewhat relentless in my quest to live life close to the bone, pulled by a longing that is larger than my desire to fit in or my fear of being rejected. This is where we get the courage to let the voice of longing speak: by letting the longing, the ache to live fully, grow larger than our fears. The voice in "The Invitation," the voice Jeff heard in that canoe thirty years ago, is the part of me that has always felt that there is an inherent if implicit meaning to our lives that is accessible, that can be known even if it cannot be readily articulated, that can offer us the wisdom we need in our daily choices. When I was fifteen, this was a hope and a hunch fueled by dreams and desires. As I approach fifty, it has become a deep conviction rooted in faith and reinforced with the direct if not always constant awareness of the Sacred Mystery, which is paradoxically both what I am and larger than myself. The difference between now and then, between fifteen and fifty, is that I am now more able to accept who I am. I no longer berate myself for the lost prom dates, no longer cringe at the odd looks I get at family gatherings or the occasional social event I attend when I ask a question that seeks to reach beyond "What do you do?"

Long before I was a somewhat peculiar teenager, I was an odd little girl. I look to my childhood now not so much to understand my development as to glean bits of wisdom about what worked then and will still work now to develop and strengthen our connection to our deepest self and the meaning in our lives. My parents gave me the two things I think we all need at any age to cultivate our inner life: a place of belonging and empty time alone. The first, a place of belonging, gives us a sense of solid ground beneath our feet, reminds us of what we can rely upon when we are tempted to let fear determine our choices. My sense of belonging came from being part of a family that loved and cared for me even when they must have wondered at my strange preoccupations. It also came from living close to the wilderness of northern Ontario. The lakes and rocks and trees of the wilderness have always spoken to me of a home that is constant in its essence even as its form is perpetually changing. It lets me touch my place of belonging in the universe as a child of this earth. These two elements—my family's love and the presence of the starkly beautiful wilderness—gave me then and continue to give me a sense of security that is not based in the ever-changing conditions of life but is rooted in the everlasting nature of love itself and the vastness of the universe of which I am a minute but integral part.

In addition to these aspects of life that offer us access to presence of the sacred—for surely love and the immensity and beauty of the physical universe are two places where humans touch the divine—I was given the second thing needed to venture into and cultivate the inner life: empty time and space. Mine was not a childhood of nightly lessons and enrichment programs. Mine was a childhood of time and space to wander, of creating new worlds through reading and writing and daydreaming. We had one television station with programming that was dominated by hockey games and critiques of the news, shows that held little appeal for a young girl. While I was introduced to the ideas of God and faith through my local church and our nightly family dinner table discussions, these ideas were offered nondogmatically. Questions were encouraged and not always answered but left to sit and grow.

The imagination is the doorway into the inner life. Mine was allowed to meander and flourish. I remember one game in particular that I played from the time I was about nine years old. I would stand somewhere alone, perhaps in my room or outside in a wooded area, with my eyes closed and turn around, stopping when I had lost all sense of which direction I was facing. Then I would open my eyes and let myself focus at random on something in front of me. It could be anything: a leaf, a blade of grass, a piece of stray garbage, a lamp, the floral pattern in my curtains, the spine of a book next to my bed. And the task I set for myself, the game I played, was to make up a story that would use whatever my eyes had settled upon as a metaphor for some lesson about life. I probably didn't even know what a metaphor was. I thought of what I was doing as making up "sermons" like the ones I heard the minister give every Sunday in church. And I never doubted for a minute that any item could be used to teach some lesson about life or that my imagination would be up to the task of

As the song reminds us,
that which feeds bodies and
souls must include both
bread and roses.

cocreating such a lesson with any item that presented itself. I would open my eyes and focus on whatever came into view—a pine cone—and begin with, "A pine cone can teach us about life . . . ," letting my imagination run to something like, "To fulfill its purpose, to release its seeds so that new trees can grow, it has to open, to unfold. . . ." You get the idea. Sometimes I wrote the stories down, and sometimes I simply told them silently to myself. I'm not claiming that I received any particularly startling insights about life by doing this. But it was never about the content, about achieving results. It was about finding connections and feeling the thrill of stretching my imagination to create meaning out of whatever was in front of me. When I think of this game now I am struck by the thread of holographic thinking that lay behind it, the unspoken certainty that all things contain the wholeness of life and are available to our imagination's ability to create and touch the meaning at the core of life.

I can see in the creation of this game a blending of my own innate love of ideas with my parents' value for things that are useful. I wanted to know, to imagine, to cocreate not only meaning from the ordinary things of life, but meaning that was useful, that presented "lessons," guidance on how to live and love well. In many Native American traditions there is an explicit appreciation for ideas that are useful, ideas that are said to help us "feed the children" or "grow corn." This valuing of practicality does not denigrate abstract ideas about God or beauty or any of the other infinite ways the mind has of imagining the world. For, as the song reminds us, that which feeds bodies and souls must include both bread and roses. Although neither of my parents shared my love of ideas, my passion for abstract concepts and ethical dilemmas, they did not discourage me from pursuing or talking about my preoccupations. In many ways I think their ability to leave me to my own devices encouraged independent thinking and left me less susceptible to the need to garner social approval. Later attempts to engage others in discussions about these ideas were driven less by a desire to find approval than a longing to deepen my own understanding by trying to articulate my ideas to others. To communicate, I had to find the stories that shared with others my burning questions or possible answers. And of course I wanted the pleasure of shared passions, the company of fellow travelers.

In the end, that is what "The Invitation" is about: a call from one heart to others to engage in life more fully *together.* Being more at ease in my own skin now than I was when I was younger, I am more able to leave others to their way of being, less likely to try to pull those who want in this moment to talk about hockey scores into discussions about my struggle to experience and stay connected to the still and spacious center of being alive. Accepting my own desire to deepen and cultivate the spiritual aspect of life, I am more able to accept others' ways of loving the world, more at peace with my own way as no less worthy than others' no matter how socially out of sync it may seem to be at times.

But still I long for the intimacy of truly being with others, of sharing our deepest souls' desires. "The Invitation" is the voice of my soul calling to you, to myself, gently reminding us that we ache for something

more than just continuing, asking us to remember our capacity for deep intimacy, our
ability to live the meaning at the center of
our lives, to be aware of the Mystery that
can hold it all.

"The Invitation" in the World

ON THE DAY AFTER THE PARTY, the morning after I had written "The Invitation," I was composing a newsletter to send out to students who had attended the retreats and classes I had offered over the years, and I decided to include the prose poem. I did not edit or rewrite it. I have joked in more recent years that had I known that so many people were going to read it I probably would have worked on it for days and ruined it or at least dulled the edge that sought to cut through to some truth beneath our usually polite and careful inter-actions. I often sent bits of my writing out to students. I wrote almost every day, and although I had had a book published by a small Canadian press four years earlier, the idea of wider publication, of making my living doing what I loved most—writing—seemed unlikely. Growing up in a working-class family in a small northern Ontario town, I had never known anyone who had written or anyone who had even known someone who had written. Providing for my family by writing was not something I focused on or thought about. I just kept writing and sharing what I wrote while I made my living teaching classes and lead-ing retreats.

I sent off the newsletter that included "The Invitation" to the six hundred people on my mailing list. I heard back from a few who expressed their appreciation for the piece. At the time I was working on an old computer, a Mac SE. The slowness of the computer combined with my limited computer skills meant that while I had access to e-mail I did not surf the Internet. So it was several years before I found out what had been happening with "The Invitation," before I discovered the journey it had taken quite separately and independently from me. What must have happened was that people on my mailing list had sent the prose poem to friends and acquaintances through e-mail, and it had spread. By the time I got online four years later there were literally thousands of Web sites displaying "The Invitation," some in strange and novel ways with unauthorized edits and unusual credits.

The Internet indeed had
given the global villagers
the ability to reach out and
speak to one another.

Slowly, as people began to track down who I was and where I lived, stories of how the poem had traveled began to trickle back to me. A woman in Africa wrote and told me that she had heard the poem read at a United Nations gathering there. Several people who had heard it at a spiritual gathering of about eight hundred people in New Zealand wrote asking for copies. I received e-mails from people in Iceland and Romania, South Africa and England, and from all over the United States and Canada. The Internet indeed had given the global villagers the ability to reach out and speak to one another.

In the midst of the stories about how the prose poem had come into people's lives, I also heard about the assumptions and speculations that were being made about who I was. One man who had attended a men's retreat with Robert Bly wrote to me of his experience of hearing "The Invitation" read by one of the retreat participants. The several hundred men in attendance had responded in unison to each stanza with an enthusiastic "Ho!" the heartsound used in traditional Native American ceremonies to indicate "that speaks for me also!" To his credit, he did not seem at all perturbed to learn I was a woman, and he felt that none of the men at the retreat would have felt less enthused in their response to the piece had they known my gender at the time. Similarly, I heard from a man who attended a weekly men's group in California where they began each meeting by reading "The Invitation." Although they had assumed I was a man, they continued to use the poem even after they found out I was a woman, and I was touched to be included in this way in their circle.

Perhaps not surprisingly, given that the piece had gone out under my medicine name, many people who read the prose poem assumed I was Native American. In fact, at the end of one version circulating on the Internet, someone had added the title "Indian elder" after my name. The culprit, a man from Chicago, wrote to me after the publication of the book *The Invitation* and confessed. Seeing my medicine name after the poem, he had assumed both that I was Native American and that I was a man, and he had added the epithet as a way of honoring the heritage he assumed I had. When he'd opened the book he'd been shocked to see my picture and had written to explain and apologize.

Someone sent me a copy of a newsletter put out by a Native band council in northern British Columbia. The newsletter had included "The Invitation" and claimed it as being "by one of our own." I was mortified that people would think I had misrepresented myself. Having been given and continuing to receive so much—including a practice that had restored my health—from the teachings and ceremonies of the Native American elders with whom I had studied, I was well aware of the understandable controversy among some concerning non-Natives learning these teachings. Too often in this profit-driven culture, the symbols and language of these ancient and sacred traditions have been used by a few as trappings for selling something or claiming an exotic and mysterious status for themselves. As someone whose life has been changed by the rigors of traditional ceremonies that require long periods of fasting and solitude in the wilderness, I too cringe when I hear people claiming a weekend retreat at a spa or a night spent outside in their urban backyard as a "vision quest"!

Years ago, I worked with a Native elder who was then living in Toronto. One day Gladys said, "You are one hand from the full blood in your family." By "one hand," she meant five generations. In her tradition it is believed that certain proclivities and abilities recur every five generations. I asked her what she was talking about, but she just smiled and said, "Go on, start digging through your family history, and you will find out I am right. It has been buried by shame."

"Gladys," I said, "why would you even think a thing like that? Look at me. I am fair-haired and blue-eyed. My ancestors came from Germany and Scotland."

"Oh, I have grandchildren who are blue-eyed," she said with a dismissive wave of her hand. She looked at me and leaned forward, "How long have you been studying these medicine teachings?"

"Five years," I replied.

She leaned back and smiled. "When you have been learning and practicing these ceremonies for sixty years, as I have, you will be able to tell a few things just by looking at a person." She reiterated her directive to research my family tree. To tell the truth, I thought she was just trying to come up with an explanation she could live with for why this crazy white girl was willing to do so much ceremony, had so much passion for learning the earth-based teachings she had learned as a child.

I completely forgot about Gladys's comment until one day a couple of years later. On this day my mother, who was less than thrilled about her daughter going off for days alone to fast in the wilderness and participating in practices that must have seemed to her to be strange if not downright dangerous, said with some annoyance, "Well maybe you do all this crazy stuff because Grampa Hildreth was Native."

I was stunned. This was the first time I had ever heard of this possibility. Turns out the family story, buried as Gladys had claimed by the shame that racism breeds, was that my great-grandfather's mother had been a Native woman from the Canadian west. If the story is true I would be five generations (this woman, my great-grandfather, my grandfather, my mother, and me)—or one hand—from her. I have not pursued proving or disproving the story. On one level it does not matter. Although I would feel nothing but pride to claim ancestry among people who lived so close to and in harmony with the earth, even if I am five generations from a full-blooded Native American ancestor I do not think this would alter the context in which I have lived. In a culture that unfortunately often offers opportunities based on skin color and cultural background, I am a white woman from an Anglo-Saxon working-class family. This is the reality I grew up with, and it is a reality that is worlds away from those who grew up on often impoverished reservations or were removed from their families and shipped off to residential schools where they were forbidden to use their language, practice their spirituality, or express their cultural heritage. To claim to be Native American, even if I could prove my family's story of heritage, would be to diminish and dishonor the suffering that has been endured by so many.

I honor what I have been given through the teachings and the ceremonies—including my medicine name—not because of my bloodline, whatever that might be, but because these practices honor the sacredness of life and have enabled me to more consistently touch the Mystery within and around me. And I accept that forces beyond my control, those mysterious powers of timing and the unexpected speed and ease of information exchange through the Internet, have sent me

The journey of "The Invitation"
has taught me about letting
go of control or, perhaps
more accurately, about
realizing how little control
I really have over many things
that affect my life.

into the world with a name that has led some to the wrong conclusions.

This is just one of the many ways in which the journey of "The Invitation" has taught me about letting go of control or, perhaps more accurately, about realizing how little control I really have over many things that affect my life. Initially my sons and I sent e-mails to people who had posted the prose poem on their Web sites with pictures of Native elders in full headdress and the epithet "Indian elder" after my name, trying to clear up the confusion. Many posted my explanation of my heritage and my disclaimer that I am neither old enough nor wise enough to be considered an elder of any people but left the title of Indian elder and the incongruous images on their sites. It quickly became apparent that we could not keep up with the number of sites that were posting the poem. My sons took great glee in exploring new

Internet territory daily and calling me to
come and see new and sometimes truly
bizarre sites where the prose poem was dis-
played. I finally decided to simply be grateful
that so many were finding something in my
writing that spoke to them, and I let go of
even trying to control how the piece was
presented.   [79]

   Although it made some sense to me that
people thought I was Native American, I was
less able to understand those who took it
upon themselves to change words in the
prose poem, editing it to suit their own ideas.
I suppose it is my own reverence for the
written word that made this cavalier editing
of someone else's work incomprehensible
to me. But over time, although I made cor-
rections where possible, I came to understand these anonymous edits as part of the
conversation the poem was having with the
world. The most common changes were

the exchanging of the word *faithless* for *faith-ful* in the stanza about betraying another to be true to oneself and switching the word *Beauty* for *God* in the stanza about sourcing our life daily. I understood both edits but insisted where I could on restoring the original. *Faithless* is an uncomfortable word. I wanted to be clear that breaking a promise to another, while sometimes necessary for our very survival, should never be done easily, should always feel uncomfortable if we are to be honorable people. I also wanted to point to a very real and hard insight I had had one day: that those I could truly trust to be who they were with me were those who might break a promise to me someday, would be those I might see and feel in that instance to be faithless.

As to the term *God,* it is, as the Jewish theologian and philosopher Martin Buber pointed out in *I and Thou,* an overburdened word, a word that carries with it all the misdeeds and atrocities that have been committed in its name. And yet I could see why some might want to remind us of the larger source of the Beauty that lifts us up daily.

Sometimes the inability to control how the poem was presented or where it was used resulted in new revelations, delightful surprises. One young woman in Russia wrote me that her boyfriend who lived in Germany had come across someone's German translation of "The Invitation." He had translated it into Russian and sent it to her, and she had translated it back into English, a language she was just learning to read and write. It was like that old game of telephone where a circle of children whisper a phrase from one person to the next, eager to see how the final version resembles or differs from the original. What I remember is the first stanza of the prose poem as she had translated it. Where I had written *I want to know what you ache for,* she had translated it as *I want to know what you shout inside yourselves for,* her words hinting at the complexity that sometimes causes confusion when different aspects of the self cry out from longings that are sometimes so disparate they seem mutually exclusive.

Stories continued to come in about where the prose poem was being used. People found beautifully printed copies propped in front of place settings at wedding receptions, heard it read by the valedictorian at their high school graduation, listened in tears as it was read at the graveside of a loved one. Therapists set copies out in their waiting rooms, recovery groups read it aloud together at the end of meetings, and speakers recited it in keynote addresses at conferences on everything from modern medicine to UFOs. In part I think because I live in Canada, I was completely unaware of most of this, did not know about the incredible journey this small piece of writing was taking until the whole things had been under way for several years.

Then one day I received a phone call from Joe Durepos, an American literary agent who was working at the time on behalf of Jean Houston. Jean wanted to include "The Invitation" in her upcoming book, *A Passion for the Possible,* and I readily gave my consent. Joe asked me what else I had written. Since the publication of *Confessions of a Spiritual Thrillseeker* in 1990 I had done a lot of writing but had not been able to find a structure for another book. Joe asked me if I had thought of writing a book based on "The Invitation." The minute he said it I knew the prose poem offered the elusive structure I had been seeking. And so, expanding upon the writing I had accumulated, I began to unfold the prose poem, using separate chapters to go deeper into the longing expressed in each

Mine is not a war story of endless effort. It is a story of ease and unearned blessings.

stanza. Joe became my agent and sold the manuscript to HarperSanFrancisco, and it subsequently became an international best-seller and was translated into over fifteen languages. The folks at Isabella Catalogue created a beautiful poster of the piece, and Laith Al-Deen, a German pop star, wrote a song based on the translated lyrics for a CD produced by Sony World. All this from a few lines written late at night after a party!

When authors seeking to get their manu-script published contact me asking for advice about how to find an agent or a publisher, I find myself cringing a little when I tell this story. Stories abound of great works of litera-ture and best-selling books that were turned down by dozens of agents and publishers before they went out into the world, stories to bolster the spirits of writers who are con-sidering papering their rooms with rejection slips. But mine is not a war story of endless effort. It is a story of ease and unearned blessings, for which I am grateful every day. The publication of *The Invitation* and the subsequent books *The Dance* and *The Call,* which complete a trilogy about the journey into a spirit-centered life, have enabled me to live the joy of writing for a living. Most days, I tell you honestly, it feels like a miracle.

With the publication of *The Invitation,* HarperSanFrancisco sent me on the road for a book tour, which enabled me to meet many of the readers who in their enthusiastic sharing of the prose poem had been responsible for its widespread distribution, an important factor in convincing a publisher to take a chance on an otherwise unknown author. I wanted to meet these people who had been silent champions of "The Invitation," to hear their stories, to thank them.

The stories I heard about how the words I had written had come into and affected people's lives made me laugh and cry, made me wonder about the possibility of real magic afoot in the world.

There were countless stories of romance, of partners who connected through the poem. At one of the first bookstores I visited in California, a beautiful young woman eagerly approached me holding hands with a tall, shy-looking man. They both looked to be in their early twenties. "I want to tell you a story about your poem," she began, words I would hear from hundreds of people over the next few years. "My girlfriend sent it to me on the Internet, and I loved it. I printed it out and took it over to my boyfriend's place, but when he read it he just shrugged and said, 'Yeah, okay. Doesn't do anything for me.' But when his roommate read it he thought it was great, he loved it as much as I did." She turned to the young man beside her. "This is my ex-boyfriend's roommate," she said, smiling the smile of a young woman in love, "and we're engaged to be married." We all laughed together.

It wasn't just the young who were finding the poem useful in locating potential mates. A lovely middle-aged couple, now married, had gotten to know each other by e-mail after being introduced online through mutual friends. One of the first things the man had sent the woman was the poem, and through it they connected. Occasionally I did hear of someone, usually a man, who, in an attempt to impress a potential mate, shared the poem and claimed to have written it, but as circulation of "The Invitation" increased this proved to be a risky ruse. More often women shared the poem with men and watched to see their reactions, convinced that a shared enthusiastic response would ensure future happiness. One woman, an attractive radio host who was interviewing me, told me during a brief commercial break in the broadcast that she had shared the poem the night before with a man she had been seeing recently. It had been their third date. She told me that when she read him the poem and he said, "I say *yes!* to all of it," she knew this was the man for her.

I loved hearing these stories, and heaven only knows I and others have gotten together with potential mates on flimsier evidence than mutual enthusiasm for writing we find meaningful. However, I admit I wondered if asking someone who is obviously interested in getting to know you in the biblical sense what they think of a poem you clearly feel is important is likely to elicit anything but a positive and enthusiastic response. But then, given the role "The Invitation" has played in my life in enabling my husband, Jeff, to find me after thirty years of separation, who am I to question the ways the universe has of bringing us together with others?

Not surprisingly, I suppose, some of the longing stirred by the poem was directed toward me as a potential partner. Before the book came out, when many still thought I was a man, I received countless notes and cards containing thinly veiled proposals and propositions from women, addressed to "Mr. Mountain Dreamer." I would write back telling them I was a woman and telling them not to feel bad, that if I thought a man had written a piece that so closely mirrored my own heart's longing, I'd have written him myself. When the book *The Invitation* came out I began to receive inquiries from men who were interested in meeting me. Most were touching testaments to the tender creatures men are and to the longing for intimacy we all share, although I admit that some were

The poem and the book
were both fueled in part by my
longing for a life partner who
would be able to enter into
deep intimacy with me.

written in a style or with an edge that betrayed a stunning lack of knowledge about women and how to woo them.

In fact, the poem and the book were both fueled in part by my longing for a life partner who would be able to enter into deep intimacy with me. I knew that although the letters I was receiving were sincere, I also knew that the level of projection these men quite naturally had sent my way after reading the book would make any possibility of a real human relationship between us unlikely. One of the lovely things about being with Jeff, someone who knew me before the days of "Oriah Mountain Dreamer and The Invitation," is that he knows and loves the human woman I am, knows I cannot always live up to the wisdom expressed in the book, cannot always let the longing in the poem guide my action.

There were, in addition to the lighthearted stories of romance, harder stories about how the prose poem had come into and affected some lives. At one of my first bookstore appearances a young woman approached me with a handmade plaque bearing the words of "The Invitation." She told me how her sister had committed suicide a year before, how she had not known how she would be able to continue in the midst of the grief and pain, had considered taking her own life. A friend had given her the poem, and she had written it out and placed it beside her bed, reading it over and over when the darkness felt unbearable. "I do not think I would be here if it had not been for these words," she told me, choking back tears.

At first, when people would tell me stories of how the prose poem or the books had helped them through a difficult time, I felt uncomfortable. Several women came to events and told me about receiving the prose poem or one of the books just before or after the death of a child, of how they'd found the words to be what they had hung on to in order to take the next breath, to live through the next day without their son or daughter. I could not imagine how any words could help in the face of such pain.

One elderly woman told me of going to a café one day in despair, contemplating suicide. She did not speak to the young man who waited on her, but when she rose to leave, not having touched her cup of tea, he approached her and took his wallet out of his pocket. "You look like you are having a hard time," the young stranger told her. "I thought maybe this would help." And he took from his wallet a piece of paper that clearly had been unfolded and refolded many times. "The Invitation" was written on the paper. The woman took the page and walked outside. Standing in the sun, she read the words and started to cry.

"Those words got me through," she told me, smiling with tears in her eyes. "Thank you."

My initial inclination when I heard these stories was to push away the gratitude. I knew I could not take responsibility for what these people had received from the words I had written. I may have, on occasion, a moment of insight, but I know that if I sat down to deliberately write something I thought would comfort someone who has suffered the loss of her child or the suicide of a dear sister or the deep despair that so often overtakes human beings, I simply would not know what to write. One day, listening to one of these stories of gratitude and feeling myself pull away wanting to say, "It wasn't me," I finally got it. It's not about me! It's

The most common comment
I get from people writing to
me about "The Invitation" is
that it expresses something
they have always felt and
perhaps been unable
to articulate.

about what happens when we do our small part, when we bring ourselves to our lives as fully as we are able. When we are able to do this, if only for the hour it takes to put some words on a piece of paper, something happens that is larger than us, something that does not come wholly from us, something in which we are blessed to participate. And what we create from such moments—whether a song or a poem or an image, whether a meal or a home or a moment of being fully present with another—offers access to something that is larger than us, offers at least a fragment of the story that can hold and give meaning to our suffering and in so doing make it bearable.

When we bring ourselves completely to this moment, when we are fully with each other, we find that we are looking at another self. The most common comment I get from people writing to me about "The Invitation" is that it expresses something they have always felt and perhaps been unable to articulate. Over and over I hear, "How did you know? I feel as if someone has written about the things I think and feel that I do not tell anyone for fear of being rejected, of being found out as odd or different, as someone who wants too much."

This recognition of the self in another's story happens because we are more alike than different, all made of the same stuff, all wanting to love and be loved, to be seen for who we are, to find our happiness and live our lives fully. Strangely, unexpectedly, writing "The Invitation," allowing my own deep longing for real intimacy, has opened me to an awareness of how there is no real separation between us, how we are all part of the same sacred life force finding its way, discovering itself in the shape of the human men and women we are.

And for this and all the other blessings "The Invitation" has brought into my life, I am grateful.

Acknowledgments

I offer my heartfelt thanks to those who have made *Opening the Invitation* possible: to David Whyte, whose poem and writing exercise offered the original spark and a way to let the words flow; to my agent, Joe Durepos, for suggesting this little book; to my editor, John Loudon, and my publisher, Stephen Hanselman, for making it happen; to the team at HarperSanFrancisco—Margery Buchanan, Kris Ashley, Jennifer Johns, Jim Warner, Ralph Fowler, Lisa Zuniga, Priscilla Stuckey, and Terri Leonard—who send the words out into the world; to Kathleen Edwards for her beautiful illustrations.

For the ongoing love and support of my friends and family, I send my never-ending gratitude and wonder.

And to all those people who took the words of "The Invitation" and shared them with friends and family, who posted them on their Web sites and read them at weddings and funerals and conferences, I send you my deep gratitude. Through your willingness to share these words, to say yes to the invitation to remember together what matters, great blessings have come into my life. Thank you.

the accusation of betrayal and not
and therefore trustworthy. i want
not pretty every day. And if you ca
want to know if you can live with f
edge of the lake and shout to th
interest me to know where you liv
if you can get up after the night of
bone and do what needs to be don
me who you know or how you came t
the center of the fire with me a
where or what or with whom you ha
from the inside when all else fa
with yourself and if you truly like